The Happiness Choice

*A Journey of Healing Emotions
of My Past to Find Happiness*

Sally Gencarelli

FIRST EDITION

Developmental edit, copy edit, and proofread done by Skye Loyd, edit-guru.com.

Interior design, cover design, and typesetting done by Alan Barnett, alanbarnett.com.

ISBN 978-0-578-25182-0 (paperback)
ISBN 978-0-578-25183-7 (ebook)

www.sallygencarelli.com

To my parents—
With loving hearts, you adopted four children and gave us the best chance for a happy life. We had many advantages growing up, and I choose to remember the happy times and love and comforting support you gave me throughout my life, which have shaped me into the person I am today. I will always love and miss you.

To my daughter—
You are my greatest life blessing. I am proud of the beautiful woman you have grown up to be. Thank you for pulling extra weight at home, which allowed me to write this book. I love you!

To my spine surgeon (Dr. K.)—
Thank you for your supportive and extraordinary medical care that enabled me to live a pain-free, active life for the last twenty-five years. You gave me my life back and I am forever grateful.

The Happiness Choice

*A Journey of Healing Emotions
of My Past to Find Happiness*

INTRODUCTION

THE LIVES OF ALL PEOPLE ARE FILLED with twists and turns and the ebb and flow of blessings and joys, as well as hard times that can change us forever. My life has been no different. My joys have been many, but those times are clouded with the memories of very difficult times. A recent event, my layoff, left me shaken with feelings of insecurity and overwhelming stress. But a short time later, as I was sorting out my reaction to this event, I realized that the traumatic emotions I was feeling had been rooted within me long before.

For quite some time, I had felt like I'd fallen off the natural current of the universe and wasn't moving forward. The balance of my existence seemed to no longer include me. I was feeling small and unsupported; I lacked confidence and struggled through each day. The stress I was feeling led to restless and interrupted sleep every night. I couldn't put my finger on the exact cause of those feelings until I began to reflect on significant events that had happened to me throughout my life. It was then that I began to see how those feelings had been immersed in my subconscious since childhood.

The devastating death of my brother—the darkest, saddest time of my life—the separation of my parents, and my divorce not only affected my existence at that time, but they left emotions and feelings that stayed with me throughout my life. In addition, debilitating spine issues left me bedridden for years in my thirties, leaving scars not only on my back but also on my spirit. These occurrences in my life that I thought I had moved past left emotional problems that remained hidden within.

While I initially thought this story was going to begin at the point of my layoff, I quickly realized that I had to press the rewind button about sixty years to fully understand how I got to where I was. I had to learn to dispose of the damaging baggage in my mind so that baggage would never again have the opportunity to attach itself to me and disrupt my happiness. I had to take myself on a journey to heal many of these emotional scars so that I could finally move forward and leave the past in the past, completely detached from my new self.

This is a journey of finding myself, the real, authentic person, the person who had spent much time within others' shadows and her own, but who found her way out to stand in her own light. I had to visit hard times along the way. And while those hard times will always be a part of my story, the emotions of those times no longer define me.

To show you where I now stand, I must show you where I have been. We cannot be at the crest of the mountain without remembering the expedition to the top. Mine was a climb that began with patience and love for myself, but it progressed on the strength of the dream of the person I aspired to be. The higher I climbed, the clearer my view of that person became. My trek had many stops along the way, but each stop contained a lesson. So, to understand where I stand now, I must bring you on the entire voyage—from where I started at the base of the mountain all the way to the summit. It is the journey up the mountain that makes the joy of being at the vertex that much more meaningful.

CHAPTER 1

ADOPTION—THE EARLY YEARS

MY PARENTS LOVINGLY ADOPTED FOUR CHILDREN: my oldest brother, my sister, my youngest brother, and me, the baby of the family. I was just shy of my first birthday when my parents brought me home. I was adopted on Valentine's Day and turned one on February 20, 1961. Ever since I was old enough to understand, I have always felt fortunate and blessed to have been adopted. I believe that adoption is the most loving thing that one person can do for another person. As well, I have always been grateful that my birth mother gave me up for adoption to give me the best chance for a happy life.

When I was thirty-four, with the blessing of my parents, I initiated a search to obtain a medical background through my adoption agency. I have never desired to meet either of my birth parents, but given my back issues at that time, and a heart condition that had been detected, I was interested in attaining medical information to benefit both me and my daughter. My biological mother was the only parent found, and she requested to speak with me. I spoke with her one time on the phone and she refused to give me any medical information unless I met her. I did not want to meet her, and with that refusal, any hope for a medical history went up in smoke. I was disappointed that she held a medical background as ransom on the contingency of meeting me.

My parents gave us a wonderful life, and we were truly loved and blessed with many advantages. My dad owned a donut company in the northeast United States and worked hard at his vision, which helped him become successful. Throughout our childhood, we went on wonderful vacations, had beautiful homes, and owned a lake house in Massachusetts where we spent all of our summers swimming, water skiing, sailing (my absolute favorite), playing all kinds of beach sports, and establishing lifelong friendships. We always looked forward to the last day of school because it meant another fun summer spent at the lake.

Even though I was only two years younger than my sister, I often felt much smaller and less significant than her. I frequently felt hidden in her shadow and tried hard to be noticed. She always seemed to be in the foreground, while I was in the background. She did many things to hurt both me and my daughter throughout much of my life, which deepened my lack of faith and trust in her. That deep lack of trust continues to this day, as we no longer speak.

Of all of my siblings, my youngest brother, Frankie, and I were closest both in age (we were eleven months apart) and in every other way imaginable. Really, he was my best friend. From when we were very young, we were bonded. When we were toddlers, I remember he and I having matching red cowboy outfits, hats and all. We would gather up nuts from a tree in our backyard, stuffing our pockets full, and then sit on the sidewalk and smash them open with rocks. When we got older and were up at the lake, he would often wake me in the wee hours of the morning to go fishing with him. He was always understanding of my squeamishness about putting the worm on the hook and removing the caught fish.

When we grew a little older and moved to a beautiful new house, we often rode our bikes to a local reservoir, bringing a lunch to eat and enjoying time together. To this day when I go to that reservoir to walk with my golden retriever, I always think of Frankie. We would also walk up to the woods behind our home and meander beside a brook just talking. He was my everything growing up. I looked up to him and admired him for his various talents, but mostly for being my number one supporter and the best brother ever. While I loved my oldest brother and sister with all my heart, Frankie and I were tightly bonded as siblings.

So when Frankie got sick at the age of fifteen in 1975, events at that time and following were very difficult. His death just one year later, and the unfortunate way his illness was handled, shattered me, my remaining siblings, my parents, and our family unit. Those shattered pieces, at least for me, never mended and remained inside me. Until now, I didn't realize that those broken pieces, and the emotions that were attached to them, had lingered. They remained a part of everything I did, everything I felt, and how I would cope with tough times ahead.

CHAPTER 2

THE DEATH OF MY BROTHER

THE DEATH OF MY BELOVED BROTHER left feelings of doubt, insecurity, distrust, loneliness, and betrayal that impacted me in ways I had not realized until preparing to write this book. Frankie's illness and death were veiled in cover-ups. Many of the negative feelings and thoughts of that time evolved into long-term paradigms. For me to grow and advance into the person I was born to be, and rid myself of the emotions that were wreaking havoc on my life and mind, I had to dig deep to release these feelings.

Not only was Frankie my closest sibling, I also looked up to him and admired him. He was extraordinarily smart and was gifted with many natural talents. Frankie went to an exclusive private school up until the time he got sick. He excelled as a student, but that was just a small part of who he was and what made him special. Frankie had an unwavering zest for adventure. At his school, he was a member of the mountain climbing, skiing, and kayak clubs, and he played the trumpet in the band. Before the age of fifteen, he built his own red and white kayak. As a family, we used to go to his kayak races on weekend mornings. Frankie was also a talented keyboard player who could hear a song on the radio and play it on the piano. He excelled at the game of chess and did his best to teach it to me. Unfortunately, I was not a good student and never mastered the game as he did. Checkers was more my speed! Frankie lived such a large life as a young teenager.

When Frankie was fifteen, my mother received a call from the nurse at his school. She said that he had a bad headache and needed to be picked up. Shortly after that, he had an MRI and was diagnosed with an aneurysm. I remember him being in the hospital for a period of time with that diagnosis. I am fortunate to have his baby book, which contains several pictures of him in the hospital at that time. He came home, but it was only a short time before he began to worsen.

The brain aneurysm diagnosis was incorrect. What was seen on the MRI was actually the shadow of a tumor, or so we were told. I'm not sure when my parents knew that the diagnosis was terminal. That summer, the summer of 1975, we went on an amazing family vacation to Hawaii. It turned out to be the final vacation we would have with our entire family. I don't remember too much between that summer vacation and when he seemed to be getting sicker, early 1976, often spending most of his time in bed. At that time, we were told that he had a brain tumor and that the treatments he was receiving were to shrink the tumor. That is all that was disclosed to my siblings and me about his condition. We never knew he could die from it.

As the early part of 1976 progressed, Frankie was stationed in my parents' bed. Each of my siblings and I took turns staying upstairs to keep an eye on him. One day I brought my desk out into the hall to do my homework so I would be able to make sure he did not get up and try to go down the stairs. I went in my parents' room to check on him, but he wasn't in bed. I walked throughout my parents' master suite, looking for Frankie. I found him in the bathroom, hanging by his hands from the window curtain rod and shaking. He asked me what was wrong with him and I told him I didn't know. Carefully, I guided him back through my parents' room and safely tucked him back into bed. I don't remember anything else about that day. But as I later thought back to his question, it was clear even Frankie was in the dark about his diagnosis.

I remember the day like it was yesterday when we were told the devastating news of his actual diagnosis. Frankie had been rushed to the hospital on Monday, March 1. My aunt had taken me to an orthodontist appointment, and when we pulled into the driveway, there was an ambulance there. They were wheeling my brother out of the house on a gurney, with my mother following close behind, crying. Later that night, my remaining siblings and I were summoned to the hospital and given the news that he had brain cancer and was going to die. That night, after my brother, sister, and I had returned home, it was just us. My brother, who is four years older than I, aged nineteen at that time, had all of us sleep in the same room together in sleeping bags. I felt the support of my brother as he tried to keep us together at that difficult time.

Frankie was in a coma, so neither my siblings nor I were given the opportunity to say goodbye and to tell our brother how much we loved him. Four days later, on the morning of March 4, 1976, we were at the hospital but not in his room when Frankie died. He was sixteen. The sadness was overwhelming and numbing. Even though family and friends were present, I have never forgotten the feeling of being completely alone in the world at that moment.

After Frankie's passing, no support was given to my remaining siblings or me, as a family unit. We were not allowed to talk about Frankie's death. For at least six months following his passing, all the shades and curtains at our house remained closed 24/7, and we were still setting a place for Frankie at the dinner table. This was a very dark time. I often cried alone in silence. I didn't have anyone to talk to about the pain and sadness I was feeling. It is still hard for me to comprehend, all of these years later, how poorly this time was managed. My parents were too engrossed in their own grief to give any thought to the overwhelming sadness of their other children.

I never felt like I was enough after that—not enough to have been taken care of during that time. Just not enough. I began to have only myself to rely on. Our family unit became dysfunctional and was never the same after Frankie's death. So much of that time is a blur to me. I think I have subconsciously buried my memory of it. Maybe not a bad thing, until now.

The death of my brother was absolutely the darkest, most difficult time in my life. It altered the trajectory of my life and changed everything. I felt alone, let down, and betrayed by my parents. Over the years, I learned that nearly everybody knew about Frankie's terminal diagnosis—everybody but the ones who should have, his own siblings. I still don't understand how nobody slipped. I learned from my mother many years later that Frankie's doctors told my parents that if they didn't reveal his diagnosis to us, they would regret it for the rest of their lives. I know that at least my mother did. On my mother's death bed, when I was alone with her as she was passing from breast cancer, she apologized to me for hiding his diagnosis. I accepted her apology but still have never understood it, and I don't think I ever will.

A few years later, another event would grind in the same emotions and feelings I felt from the loss of my brother. A hidden disruption to my weakened family dynamic not only caused a break to occur in the relationship of my parents, but it climaxed in a breaking point for me.

CHAPTER 3

THE SEPARATION
OF MY PARENTS

ABOUT TWO AND A HALF YEARS after the death of Frankie, my parents separated. The feelings from my brother's passing were still raw, so this event compounded those sentiments. It wasn't the split of my parents that was difficult for me to cope with, it was the manner in which I discovered this news that caused me to slowly unravel and spiral out of control. After Frankie's death, I became very withdrawn and quiet, but my reaction to my parents' separation was quite the opposite.

Just two weeks prior to my going away to start college in August 1978, I was walking around the corner into our kitchen and stopped as I heard my parents talking. I hid out of sight and eavesdropped on their conversation. This is how I learned of their impending separation. I barged in on them and loudly shared my opinion about what I had just heard. I was angry and hurt by the way I found out. We never sat down as a family to communicate with each other about this disruption to our family.

Just as with my brother's death, we were expected to go on as usual. But my family's usual was anything but usual. My parents' dysfunctional way of coping with any topic that was uncomfortable continued. Nothing was learned from events surrounding Frankie's death. It seemed that anything that would involve dealing with emotions was taboo with my parents. We were never encouraged to talk about our feelings. It was impressed on us that emotions and feelings should be felt inside and left inside. I proceeded through life with those same notions.

College life started out well but quickly spiraled in an unpleasant direction. While I escaped from my feelings of sadness, distrust, and anger within the walls of my home, that emotional baggage didn't stay in its place. I started to rebel and it wasn't pretty. I was drinking—not tremendously, but enough to let my studies go by the wayside. I withdrew from college at Thanksgiving and moved back home.

My parents thought I was being difficult and took no responsibility for their actions, or non-actions, from the time of Frankie's death and beyond. I never got any help to resolve my emotional issues. I could not escape the darkness that overtook me living in our home. The memories from Frankie's loss and feelings of him being around me, coupled with having to be around my dad's girlfriend, were too much, so I took the drastic measure of escaping. Under the strong disapproval of my parents, I went to Utah.

I had a friend who was going to college out there and had an apartment with a vacancy, so I took it. I sowed many wild oats and had a lot of fun in the two years I spent in the beehive state, but there was always something not right about me. I was having fun on the outside, but on the inside I was drowning. I kept on running to escape from something that there was no escape from— an extreme sadness and I suppose depression. Even after I came home, I remained rebellious and did everything I could to hold up the wall between my parents and me.

From the outside, nobody could have known what was going on within me. I looked happy, had friends and boyfriends, and probably resembled others of my age group. But in retrospect, I felt small, untrusting, and withdrawn, and I never aspired to anything more than what was in my small world. I had no one whom I could rely on to talk about how I was feeling. When I shared this manuscript with a few friends to get their feedback, one of them, whom I had met when I was seventeen (not long after my brother died), said she never knew that I had felt like this.

I continued having a low self-esteem and hiding my inner self from the world. But when I was twenty-four, I met someone who changed things. A guy who seemed to be good for me. He felt different. I shared more of myself with him than probably anyone up to that time. He would eventually be my husband and give me one of my greatest gifts, my daughter. "Seemed" was a feeling that often got me in trouble. I always seemed fine, but I wasn't. While this guy seemed to be good for me, he disrespected, deceived, and hurt me in an unspeakable way.

CHAPTER 4

COURTSHIP, MARRIAGE, DIVORCE

THE RELATIONSHIP I HAD WITH MY THEN-HUSBAND varied from really good to tumultuous. There were times when he would do anything for me, and then he would turn around and hurt me. And I accepted that. At that time, except for Frankie and a few friends, that was how most of my relationships were. Sad, but true. But I could never have seen how hurtful the end of our relationship would be.

We dated for four years before getting married. In the early part of our relationship, he was an undercover security guard for live events at several local arenas. I saw many amazing concerts, as he was able to get tickets for shows. They were a lot of fun. My all-time favorite musician is Bruce Springsteen, and in 1984, my boyfriend got me a ticket to see the "Born in the U.S.A." tour. I screamed so much in that concert, I lost my voice for four days. It was awesome! Those were great times with wonderful memories, but the wonderful memories were snuffed out several years later.

Just a few weeks prior to our planned wedding on April 29, 1988, we found out I was pregnant. We were happy about the news but kept it quiet until after the wedding. That pregnancy ended in a miscarriage. The month that we were able to start trying again, I got pregnant. Although my husband seemed happy about that news, he was about to turn my world upside down.

Just a few months into the pregnancy, he announced that he was seeing someone else and moved out. I was devastated, to say the least. It is hard to describe all of the emotions I was feeling at that time. But *betrayed* was at the top of the list. I went through the entire pregnancy alone. The person that I gave my all to and trusted hurt not only me but most importantly our child. We were deceived in such a cruel way.

He was not there when she was born. It was recommended by my lawyer to not file for divorce until after she was born. While I invited him to come and see her prior to the divorce, he declined. He first met her when she was four months old. He has been in and out of her life for her whole life. At thirty-one years old, she now makes the effort to visit him and his wife once a week. The way he has hurt her breaks my heart. It was never about me; I only worried about my daughter.

I have been divorced for thirty-one years and have never remarried. I hid the emotions from that time because I didn't want the focus to be on me, I wanted it to be on my child. The way in which I was hurt and deceived is something that has stayed with me, and I have never been able to trust another man to give my whole self to. Maybe some day.

Masking my emotions has plagued me much of my life, but I was soon to travel through a multiyear period of time that would have me hiding both emotional and physical pain.

CHAPTER 5

HIDING THE PAIN

RECENTLY, I WAS TELLING SOMEONE ABOUT the events surrounding the death of my brother, and tears were streaming down my face, though my brother left this earth in 1976. It was a very long time ago in years, but not long at all in my heart. It was an enormous burden to carry all of these emotions and feelings of being small, invisible, unworthy, and untrusting for my entire life.

Although it caused troubles that reverberated for years, I believe that my parents did what they thought was best when they made the decision to hide my brother's diagnosis from Frankie, my siblings, and me. Or perhaps, even with their separation, they were too immersed in their own sadness to give thought to ours. I don't think they could have understood the ramifications of burying those emotions and feelings. While my early life was hard, my mom and dad did develop into caring, loving, and attentive parents and grandparents as I got older. I accepted and appreciated their outpouring of support and love through some very difficult times. Their kindness and support are what I choose to remember.

My mom was nurturing to me at the times when I needed it the most. When my first pregnancy ended in miscarriage, my parents were very supportive of me. Anybody who has gone through a miscarriage knows how difficult it is. The day that I learned the fetus I was carrying did not have a heartbeat, I experienced an emotional earthquake. I didn't call either of my parents until the next day to tell them. When I called my mother and told her, she cried. No sooner had I hung up the phone, there was a knock at my door, and my mother was there to offer her support and comfort to my husband and me, as only a mother can.

When my daughter was born, she couldn't have been happier for me. It was a hard time emotionally for me because I was alone and I held much of that in. But my mother was there for me in every way. My mom showered my baby and me with gifts and attention before and after the birth. She stayed with us for the first two weeks after little Erica came home. She was a loving mom and grandmother, and we appreciated all of her love and support.

In my late twenties, shortly after my daughter was born, I began to experience intermittent back pain. My mom was very caring when my back hurt. She would often come over on a Sunday, pick up our laundry, and bring it back to me the next day washed and folded. Just hearing her on the other end of the phone when I wasn't feeling well was comforting. As well, she often would invite us over for dinner or bring dinner over to us. Her kindness, compassion, and attentiveness were very meaningful and appreciated by my daughter and me.

In my early to mid thirties, 1992 to 1994, the pain levels in my back varied from moderate to debilitating. I slowly began to fall emotionally into dark times. I was functional up to a point, but when I was home, my time was spent in bed. As my pain progressed, I began to shut myself off from the world. I was in too much discomfort to want to do anything outside of the realm of my home and often my bed. This time was made even harder by my status as a single mom with a seven-year-old daughter. I often felt guilt that my daughter's life was being affected by my limitations. It was a hard time for both of us.

I had a small inner circle that I had to rely on for everything. My mom passed away the year before my first spine fusion surgery, so I didn't have her supportive presence surrounding me. However, she did make her presence known to me: I often felt her comforting energy surrounding me. My dad did his best to be there for me at that time. He often would come over and just sit by my bed. It was reassuring knowing that he was there. My dad took me to all of my doctor's appointments and often would pick up Erica on Saturdays to take her out for a while. Friends also helped with my daughter. My biggest concern at that time was not for myself but my young child. It was a hard balance being honest with her regarding my condition while giving her assurance that everything would be okay. She was much too young to be burdened with worry.

As much as possible, I tried to involve Erica with doctor's appointments with my surgeon. It was important to me that she develop a sense of faith in him as I did. I wanted her to know that I was in the best hands possible, because I was. My surgeon was very reassuring to her throughout my many years of back problems. Little did I know at that time that he would be an enormous source of support to both her and me as she traveled through her own back problems several years later.

I tried to make her life as normal as possible throughout this time. She was allowed to have friends over to play or to sleep over, occasionally. As well, she often was invited on overnight visits to her friend's homes. My bed often resembled a playground, as we would play games and do her homework on it. No matter how I was feeling, I always got out of bed on school mornings to keep a normal routine. Eating breakfast with her, making her lunch, and preparing her for the day gave us a normalcy that one would imagine for any family. A helpful neighbor would bring her to the school bus stop every morning, meet her at the bus stop in the afternoon, and walk her home. Once she settled at home after school, the rest of most days and evenings were spent on my bed. She certainly fell behind in areas of her development, but I did my absolute best in the situation I was in.

Living with chronic pain brings more than simply physical challenges; the emotional struggle is just as debilitating. My restrictions were enormous physically and socially. My mobility was extremely limited, and eventually, it became excruciating just to lie in bed. Breathing in too deep would often make me cry. The isolation and loneliness of this time and needing to rely on my small inner circle for everything was depressing. I spent much of my alone time enveloped in overwhelming sadness over my situation. I became withdrawn and eventually depression set in.

Even though this was a very difficult time, I somehow never lost hope that it had to get better. Crippling back pain could not represent my entire life; there had to be more. Throughout the many years of this period, and living in a back brace for much of the time, I kept my thoughts on a better life. One of my most liberating moments throughout this period was when I was allowed to drive for the first time after being flat on my back for six months recovering from my first spine fusion. My doctor had told me that I could drive around town; I went home that day and drove around for an hour. It was a bit of a stretch of his instructions, but I did stay within my town. It was awesome!!

I was fortunate to have been connected with my spine surgeon, who took me under his wing. After many years of treatment, and two spine fusions later, spanning from when I was thirty-two up until my mid-forties, my amazing surgeon gave me my life back.

Along with my daughter, he is one of the greatest blessings in my life. His patience, compassion, and tremendous talent as a surgeon brought me through the hardest time in my life, physically. I can't even fathom where I would be without him.

While my back healed to the point where I slowly was able to regain activity, the emotional side was much harder to recover from. I had been shut off from the world for so long that it was hard to socially and physically adjust to the life that had been gone for so long. I also held a lot in throughout this health ordeal because I didn't want to disclose to friends and family the emotional toll this time had taken on me. While people saw the effects of my pain on the outside, no one was aware of the effects of my pain on the inside, even my surgeon. It was a burden I carried by myself.

Reentering my life was a slow process, but with highs, lows, a lot of determination, and support from my surgeon, family, and friends, I claimed my life back. For the most part, the physical pain resolved. I was able to begin living a life that I had dreamed of. Most importantly, my daughter was able to have a mom who could give her the attention and life that she deserved. A turning point for us was the day that I presented her with three tickets, one for her, one for a friend of hers, and one for me, to see Destiny's Child and Christina Aguilera in concert in September 2000. She was eleven. We had the best time ever!

I held in the emotions of those years, along with those feelings I had embedded inside after the death of my brother and the events that followed his death. About twenty-five years later, these emotions and feelings would come to a climax through another life-changing crisis that rocked my world.

CHAPTER 6

MY LAYOFF

Even before the notice of my layoff made its way to me in July of 2020, life had been feeling hard. I felt stuck in an existence that had me running crazy from one responsibility to another. Work had been increasingly trying. There were stresses within my position that created stresses in my personal life. I was the administrative assistant for the oncology genetics program at a local hospital. Working in oncology brought emotional stresses, as we had certain cases where the emotions were hard to not take home. Management was shifting, affecting the energy that encompassed my position. I no longer felt like my efforts were appreciated. It was hard for me to leave the uneasiness I felt in my gut at work when I logged out and left the building. It took all of my inner strength to get through the work shift, leaving me little energy for the remainder of the day.

I was juggling and balancing all of my responsibilities, but I no longer seemed to be a part of that balance. I was lost. Those familiar feelings of being small, in a shadow that I could not find my way out of, with anxiety that had me feeling insignificant, were raging. It was a time of great turmoil that I could not navigate my way out of.

The anxiousness from my job was making my personal life hard. Friendships were being affected, as I often canceled on commitments with friends because I was so exhausted and strained. My existence was becoming difficult. I was almost looking at myself as a separate being and not recognizing the person I was observing. My mind and self were never present in the moment I was in; my thoughts were always racing around what I needed to do. All the relationships in my life were affected, most importantly the relationship with myself.

I was going through the motions when I was not clocked in at work, but they were just motions. I was very good at managing my responsibilities at work and in my personal life, but I was crashing at managing myself. The stress was building up and taking a toll on me. Sleep, what sleep?? I was getting no more than two hours of sleep a night, as my mind was always filled with worry and anxiety. I was being stretched in many directions and often snapped from my stresses. I kept up with life the best I could, but I was slipping into an uncomfortable place. A silent depression over my state of being was seeping in. I didn't have the strength or energy to see a way out of this turmoil. But the universe was about to step in and help me out.

As I was away from work for much of the time leading up to my layoff, courtesy of shoulder surgery recovery and being furloughed, I was feeling calmer and enjoying my abundance of free time. Stresses were lessening, and I was feeling lighter and more carefree. My golden retriever, who I think was under the impression that I had quit my job to stay home with him, was thrilled to have Mom home more. Life was feeling better. But there was always a dark cloud hanging over my head: the thought that I was eventually going to have to return to my job.

When my layoff noticed arrived, it was met with mixed emotions. I no longer had to reenter the rat race that had wreaked havoc on my spirit, but I lost the security of my job, my salary, and the benefits that supported my family and me. That worry eased a bit when I learned of my generous severance package. As I adjusted to my new life, feelings of insecurity and anxiousness managed to seep into my mind that had disturbed my inner self for my whole life. I had to find a way to ease those troubling feelings so I could move forward to the life of peace and joy that I had glimpses of through my time of being furloughed.

To move forward, I had to trust. I had to take down all the walls I had erected around me to protect my feelings and self. I had to choose trust to be vulnerable and courageous as I immersed myself in this journey.

CHAPTER 7

PERMISSION TO TRUST

THROUGH MY LIFE'S EXPERIENCES UP TO THIS POINT, I developed a shield of caution to control who and what entered my field of energy. My heart had hardened from betrayals of trust throughout my life. I opened up to very few people because I didn't want to get hurt. But to move forward into the life I was seeing, wanting, and needing, I had to let my guard down and trust in the universe to guide me through this time. I had experienced a few times in my life where I had fully trusted and had not been deceived, and it was the reminder of those occurrences that gave me permission to have faith in trusting others.

The first person whom I completely trusted, and who didn't betray that trust, was my spine surgeon. It takes faith to allow a surgeon to operate on your spine; one wrong slip and I could have been paralyzed. But I was in no position to not trust him. I needed him and knew he would help me. He proved to me by his kindness and compassion that he had my back, literally. It was that kind of trust I needed now, where I completely let my shield down and opened myself up, fear and all, to be guided to the pain-free life I now cherish.

My golden retrievers have me taught me about opening my heart and trusting. Dogs are amazing creatures because they allow you to be vulnerable. You can share your true self without the fear of getting hurt or being judged. There is a security with dogs, or animals in general, that they are not going to betray you. When you open your heart to them, they open their heart to you, fully and completely. They teach that love should be respected, appreciated, and never betrayed, from both directions. Both of my dogs have taught me when you love hard and trust completely and unconditionally, that love and trust should be cherished, always.

I made the decision to remove all of my barriers and allow myself to be fully and completely exposed to the pilot of my journey. I placed my trust in the universe, just as I trusted my spine surgeon, to be guided out of the turmoil I felt and to lead me in the direction of lasting happiness. One step nudged me further and further through this pilgrimage of the awakening and revival of my body, mind, and spirit.

CHAPTER 8

ACCEPTANCE

ACCEPTING THAT EVERYTHING UNFOLDS IN LIFE as it is meant to and having faith and trust in life's timing have been a lesson to me throughout my life. So many events that had occurred during my life up to now had left me in a state of utter mayhem. But, as time unfolded to show me the whole picture, I was able to see and understand the why. While I have never understood the why of the loss of my brother (maybe that will be unveiled to me when I am ready to understand), I have gotten clarity on other events.

Heartbreakingly, my beloved golden retriever Kylie died in 2015 after a brief battle with cancer at the young age of eight. Kylie was too good of a dog to be lost so early, and she suffered greatly. While I grew up with dogs, she was my first dog and was intertwined in my life in a meaningful way. In some ways, she was a healer. Before Kylie came along in June of 2007, New England winters wreaked havoc on my arthritis. I had to take medication through the cold weather season to ease the pain in my joints. After my first winter with her, I realized that I had made it through the season pain free. My doctor told me it was because being out and about with her in the cold made my body adjust to the frigidness of winter. Such a gift from my special girl!

Her loss was hard, and I had a very difficult and emotional time after her passing. My grief led me to speak with a therapist, who aided me in moving forward. It was the first time I had ever outwardly expressed my feelings of sadness and reached out for help when I was in turmoil. For a while, I didn't think I could fall in love with another golden retriever. Thinking back, it wasn't until my counselor helped me to resolve my emotions surrounding her passing that my heart began to feel ready for another golden puppy. Accepting her loss allowed me to uncover the blessing that would soon follow.

Nine months later, I welcomed to my heart and life my sweet Colby, about whom you will hear much more in the coming pages. When I first held him at five weeks old, there was no doubt that he was born just for me. He seemed to fit perfectly in my arms. When Colby came home, he walked into his new house with confidence, fit in immediately, and never looked back. For Kylie, it took two weeks for her to settle and adjust to her new surroundings. There were a few signs that he was meant to be mine. His dad is from Kylie's breeder, and when I told his breeder the name I had chosen for him, I was told that his great grandfather was also named Colby. If Kylie hadn't died, I most likely would not have him. But the feeling that he was born for me made it clear that Kylie's passing was a natural succession in life. She made room in my heart for Colby. While I miss her every day, I am so thankful for her time with me, and for the little boy that she paved the way for. Just as accepting the timing of Kylie's passing brought me the gift of Colby, I needed to do the same for my layoff. I had to begin to accept the past to uncover the blessings that were ahead of me.

When I first received my layoff notice, I was filled with uncertainty and was a jumbled, stressed mess. But as I began to process my position being eliminated, I tried to be patient with the emotions that I was feeling. Just as we mourn when we lose a loved one, I had to allow myself time to acknowledge my feelings about this loss. I began the process of accepting this severe disruption in my life but intentionally did not let these emotions define me. I recognized and accepted them so I could eventually find the strength to move on. I had to be careful to not allow these reactions to my layoff to be buried in my subconscious and thus follow me throughout my life. I have learned my lesson about that. I was aware of them but did my best not to focus on them. I have learned that thoughts and emotions are energy, and the more power we give to those energies, the stronger the energy gets. An important lesson there!

Acceptance of my layoff began to lead me to thoughts of what the universe was making room for in my life. It was time to figure out how to navigate my way through this time of uncertainty to a place where I could look for the opportunities of the future. Leaving the past in the past, releasing all of the negative and limiting feelings and ideas deep inside of me, and uncovering the self-confidence and courage to believe in the greatness that I was born for was now my mission. Sometimes our greatest blessings can come from our biggest challenges, and I was determined to uncover the blessings that lay ahead. My challenges were to be placed in the background, and in the foreground would go the faith that I would find my greatest self on the other side of this voyage. Detaching myself from the negative feelings and emotions of the past would allow me to dream and move toward the future.

Since my way hadn't worked so well leading up to this time, I began to realize that I had to release my white-knuckle grip on the steering wheel of life. My steering wheel, the Italian stubborn one, led me to unfavorable circumstances that had me feeling like life was hard. To reverse this cycle, I had to allow the universe to lead the way. While I had been feeling like I was swimming against the current of life, slipping back instead of moving ahead, I finally was beginning to feel more like I was treading water. A definite improvement! Although I don't react well to change, life presented this change and I had to find a way to adjust. I have also learned through this time that when you resist something it persists, so I had to stop resisting it and let it be. My layoff became a welcomed interruption that I began to appreciate more and more.

When my thoughts would veer back to the panic and worry that my layoff brought, I would try to place my faith in the universe. As that faith grew, I began to feel more calm and relaxed. Having the cushion of my severance package contributed to the ease of my anxious nerves. The process of accepting my layoff allowed me to continue to develop a state of peace and to feel like the universe was taking care of me. This time also allowed me to continue my shoulder surgery recovery, which was still a big part of day to day living.

For several weeks, I had appointments every day for my shoulder, from physical therapy to a laser treatment I was receiving. Having this time available to continue these treatments was valued. I was grateful to be able to give my shoulder the best shot at a successful recovery. This realization was beginning to give meaning to the timing of my layoff.

Eventually being okay with how things were and finding little things to be thankful for helped to increase my faith in the universe and my trust in the ups and downs of life. There were a lot of ebbs in 2020, for me and the rest of the world. Accepting the ebbs allowed the worry to flow away. I began the process of respecting these natural movements of energy and looked toward the regrowth that would spark my journey of lifting myself to new heights.

As I continued to allow myself to be guided through this time, I felt more in harmony with the flow of life. Even with that trust, intermittent thoughts of what I had lost through my layoff still plagued me. I began to focus on an attitude of gratitude to redirect my thoughts to what I had instead of what I had lost. It was gratitude that began to change my paradigm of focusing on the negatives to focusing on the positives. As I focused on my blessings, my mood and outlook began to shift.

CHAPTER 9

GRATITUDE

As I CONTINUALLY GUIDED MY THOUGHTS to acceptance of the place that I found myself in, I began to appreciate the changes I was seeing and feeling within myself and my world. Life was feeling better, a complete about-face from just a few months prior. I could hardly remember the person before my layoff. Focusing on my blessings began my journey to gratitude.

Gratitude used to be an emotion that was initiated by a gesture from another person; it was not something that originated within me. If someone gave me a gift or did something for me, I certainly said thank you. But this time of reflection began to change that. As my appreciation grew for the changes I was experiencing, gratitude became a ritual. I was alive, I was healthy, the sun was shining, and my family was healthy. There was so much to be grateful for in those four things. As my focus shifted from a zoom lens to a wide-angle lens, I was able to view my life as a whole. My awareness of everything I had to be grateful for continued to grow.

I began a new habit: every morning before I got out of bed, I typed ten things on my computer that I was grateful for. I have a document labeled "Thankful" on my Mac that I open each morning to add ten more gifts of gratitude to my list. With each entry, I added why I was grateful for that particular thing. It was not only the what, but also the why; the why gave meaning to the what. While this process began slowly, my mind now floods with things I am grateful for and I can no longer stop at just ten. As the list grew, my mood and attitude began to shift and I began to see all the positives that were present in my life to express gratitude for. My paradigm of "Woe is me" began to shift to "Happy am I!" That one document is now nine months old and has more than seventy-five thousand words. Periodically, I read through the document and truly feel how immensely blessed I am.

As my paradigms continued to shift and repetitive thoughts of loss were replaced with thoughts of acceptance, that acceptance allowed me to see what this time was presenting to me, and my gratitude grew. My life was getting bigger; I was no longer zoomed in on minor things that had no meaning or purpose. I was thankful that I did not have to jump out of bed and race around to get to work on time to a job that had been a source of stress. I had a reprieve from racing a race that I never won, a race that had no finish line. I eventually expressed gratitude for my layoff because it was making me more aware of the beauty and blessings that were present in my life. Imagine that, being grateful for something that disheveled my existence to panic. I was now defining my day instead of letting outside circumstances do it. For that, I had immense gratitude.

Even as gratitude was changing my view of the world, there were times when thoughts of what I had lost took on a life of their own. I had to find a way to stay aware more often, to keep my attention on the time that I was in, rather than on the thoughts that would randomly pop into my mind. How could I find a way to control my thoughts and maintain my new focus? Meditation!

CHAPTER 10

MEDITATION

MEDITATION WAS SOMETHING THAT I CERTAINLY HAD HEARD OF and had contemplated trying, but I had never found the time. A lack of time was an excuse I often used for not doing something—but I didn't have that excuse anymore. Being mindful of the present moment instead of the past was necessary for appreciating and expanding the place that I was now in. In an attempt to be in control of my thoughts and ignore my mind's nonstop chatter, which often insisted on dragging me into feelings of insecurity, I decided to take a leap of faith and try this technique. While it started slowly, as my concentration grew, I became quite enamored as I began to dive deeper and deeper into this mode of controlling my thoughts. Meditation was life changing and mind calming.

This practice brought with it an eventual freeness of my wandering mind. My first meditation session didn't go well and left me frustrated, as I couldn't focus my thoughts for five minutes. My golden retriever, however, seemed to have no problem with his concentration. When I opened my eyes after my first practice, Colby was lying on his back on the floor next to me, sound asleep.

As I progressed, I became so relaxed that I would often find myself falling asleep as well. The more I traveled through daily meditations, the more that I began to have better control of my attention span through focusing on the rhythm of my breathing instead of my thoughts. With that, I was able to free myself of the stresses resulting from focusing on the images and thoughts in my mind. Eventually, mindfulness began to be a dominant habit.

This practice began to train me and continues to train me on the process and energy of thoughts. Thoughts should move through our minds like balloons; they should float in and float out without focusing attention on them. The only time that thoughts can be harmful is by energizing them with the power of recognition. I began to have a deep feeling of tranquility as I changed the energy of my focus away from the thoughts in my mind to the moment I was in. There were still times when thoughts would grab my attention, but I was beginning to have the power to refuse them that energy. The more that I was able to train myself to stay in mindfulness, the happier I was. I was directed to the lessons that we humans can learn from the thought processes of dogs.

Dogs are magical creatures in so many ways. Their thoughts are only on the present, as they place no focus on the past or the future. They live for the moment they are in and nothing beyond. These special four-legged beings enjoy the simplest moments of life to the fullest. When I look at Colby, I can tell he just lives. He wags his tail in happiness over the smallest things. Our canine companions are true masters of their focus and freedom from their minds. They live how we should all live, being present in the moment and nothing beyond that, and enjoying and making the most out of the simplest things in life. Meditation began this process for me.

The more I practiced meditation, the more I was able to focus through the entire session without giving my attention to thoughts. It was noticeable within myself how meditation was calming my being. This was a big step to achieving freedom from my mind. I soon was able to meditate longer, and with that, my confidence increased, my attention span lengthened, and other areas of my life improved. As mindfulness allowed me to control overthinking, I was able to fall asleep easier, as I was able to not focus on my chitter-chattering mind. I found myself able to redirect my thoughts away from the negative emotions and thoughts that had once consumed me and enjoy the simple beauty of the present.

Before meditation, and before this time, when I would be out walking my dog, or doing anything really, I would be thinking about all sorts of things instead of the time I was in. Now, the simple task of taking Colby for a walk became a joy. I felt joy and appreciation for our time together and for the serenity that filled me as we were out and about. I was solely focused on the beauty of the world as we were walking. My continuing commitment to staying in awareness when I was moving throughout my day helped me to appreciate the small things in life. I now had the tools to turn the focus away from my mind, which removed all worry and uneasiness from my being, most of the time.

I was feeling less and less consumed by my thoughts and more appreciative and aware of the calm that replaced the stress of my overactive thoughts. The art of mindfulness freed my attention to notice things I would not have noticed before. Colby and I were out for a walk early one morning, and I noticed a leaf that was in the shape of a heart. I felt like the universe was sending love to me. When I felt that emotion from a leaf, I knew something was changing. On another early morning walk with my little guy, we encountered a pack of bikers who sped by us. My first thought was that they were missing so much as they were racing through life so quickly and not noticing the beauty of the world. It was like looking at my old self in a mirror. I was creating a new image of myself, and I liked the image I was beginning to see!

I also noticed myself being mindful of my moods. I became a much calmer person. I flew off the handle much less. One day when I was off doing an errand, I got caught in a sudden downpour. I was drenched! Before, this would have changed my energy and put me in a bad mood. But it didn't! I found myself grateful for the rain because it was a very humid day and the rain cooled me off. Being mindful of my moods, as well as my thoughts, was a huge benefit of meditation for both me and my family. Happy mom, happy home!!

This time was allowing me to relax and enjoy my life and my surroundings in a way I had never done before. To notice the intrinsic artistry of the world was transforming. This realization was a turning point for me. It supported my earlier thought that everything happens for a reason. The reason for my layoff was to permit me to slow down and be aware of the beauty of the world and allow life to show me its true meaning. Being in a marathon against life while I was working took that away from me, but I was beginning to get it back. As I committed to the present and as the stress from my layoff subsided, I began to focus more and more on what made me happy. It was time to have some fun!

CHAPTER 11

TIME FOR SOME FUN

Fun was something that had been absent from my life and thoughts for so long. But as I began to relax and stay present, I became aware of all the available time that I now had. It was time for some enjoyment. We were amid the pandemic, so it helped that it was summer and we could enjoy the natural social distancing of the great outdoors. The summer of 2020 turned out to be what I labeled "the summer of fun"!

So much to do, so many options, where should we start? The beach! While I grew up spending summers divulged in water sports and activities at our lake house, the beach was not something that I enjoyed or appreciated. When I was younger, I certainly spent time lying out on the beach, frying my skin in the sun. At the age of sixty, not so much! But I soon found out that the beach offered so much more than sunburns. I had learned of a beach where dogs were welcome, so one day we found ourselves on a road trip to the Rhode Island shore.

As we climbed the incline to the entrance to the beach, I thought that we would just walk along the beach, relax, and go home. But I quickly found myself running along with Colby as he made his way down the shoreline. Wait, what?? I am not a runner!! On that first trip, Colby brought out a side of me that I had not seen in decades. He brought out the child in me. So fun!

That one trip to the beach inspired countless adventures to our favorite coastline last summer. But this time inspired so much more than fun. Colby's zest for life wore off on my daughter and me. It energized adventure and sparked family time, which had been missing for so long. Our trips to the beach were much more meaningful when my daughter came along. My daughter, Colby, and I would make a whole family experience out of our journeys to the shore. We stopped for dinner at outside establishments, enjoyed our beach time as we walked the entire length of the beach back and forth, got ice cream, and just enjoyed the area. Often we would park ourselves in the grass and watch the sunset. The relationship between my daughter and me had been strained for some time. But our many amazing adventures at the beach sparked the beginning of the healing of our relationship, a blessing in and of itself.

Our excursions out and about sparked my adventurous side, a side of myself that had been missing for too long. My daughter and I found ourselves often planning some kind of an outing to enjoy. And what's more enjoyable than ice cream? The summer of 2020 also earned another label, "the summer of ice cream." We—I—ate more ice cream last summer than I had in my entire life. It didn't take much to twist my arm to make a trip to the ice cream stand. And this obsession didn't end as summer came to a close. Sunday night became family night out for ice cream, no matter the season we were in. My daughter, Colby, and I traveled all over Connecticut looking for the best ice cream. I could even justify ice cream as being healthy: it had protein and calcium in it, after all! Our trips for fun and ice cream were and continue to be memorable and plenty.

I began to realize that one of the things that made our outings relaxing and enjoyable was that throughout all of our excursions, we were not racing against the clock. We were out enjoying the time we were in, and it was all about the experience with no focus on what we had to do next. We were in the moment, enjoying the moment; it was not about time. The seeds that meditation planted within me were in full bloom. We completely let go of all strings tugging us in various directions. It was about one thing—family.

Colby and I enjoyed time hiking. When my daughter could come, it was wonderful; if not, it was Colby and me. We had gone hiking prior to this time, but staying in the here and now, I noticed so much more along our expeditions than I ever had before. The beauty, calmness, and vastness of Mother Nature could take my breath away. At the beach, it was the soothing reactiveness of watching the ebbs and flows of the waves as they crashed on the shore. Appreciating the absolute perfection of nature and noticing how my presence was absorbing the calming nature of all that I was seeing and feeling was amazing.

Through all of our experiences, I began to center my attention on the abundance that I was surrounding myself with. At the beach, it was the abundance of the ocean, the sky, and the seagulls. Out and about hiking, it was the abundance of trees and wildlife. In my inner self, there was an abundance of serenity. Such immense plenteousness in the world that I was seeing all around me. My life before this time was narrowly focused, but my focus was widening. As I took in this bounteousness, I would often say to myself, "May all of the abundance that I am viewing be mirrored and reflected into my life." I was beginning to feel my world open as this abundance began to fill the space inside and outside of my self.

During this time of experiencing life in such a meaningful way, I began to place an emphasis on renewing friendships. I had often canceled plans with friends using a myriad of excuses, and if I did get together with friends, while I was physically present, my mind was elsewhere. About a year and a half ago, a friendship formed with a group of high school friends. Many of those in our group weren't in the same circles in high school, but we somehow came together to form this wonderful union. It is what friendships should be, supportive and fun. We have regular get-togethers, and our time is always fun and enjoyable. Other friendships have also blossomed over this time. The renewal of friendships is one of many blessings that have come to me throughout this time of personal reflection and growth.

A focus on enjoyment had also seemed to nudge me toward family time, which brought a new harmony between my daughter and me. I began to reflect back on how many blessings came before this time as I had heeded the nudges presented to me by the universe.

CHAPTER 12

BLESSINGS FROM NUDGES

WHILE I DIDN'T THINK OF IT AT THE TIME, many of the good things that have happened in my life came through receiving nudges from the universe. The gentle whispers that knocked on my spiritual door brought me blessings, sometimes life-changing ones. At times, my strong-headed Italian stubbornness has me thinking that I know best, but thankfully I paid attention to various nudges that were presented to me. When I didn't, I learned a lesson.

I do not doubt that the timing of life brought this period to me to allow me to overcome the darkness of my past and show me the brightness of my future. Maybe I wasn't prepared previously to accept the information that I was now receiving. But the nudge, actually more like a jolt, of my layoff that I had no choice but to listen to has brought me along this time-traveling adventure that I now find myself on. I have reflected on my life to see the many nudges that redirected me to great things. My spine surgeon came to me as a result of someone who briefly entered my life and whose nudge I am so grateful I listened to.

Years ago, when I was in physical therapy for my back, a fellow patient approached me and suggested that I call the surgeon who had helped him with his back—maybe he could help me too. At first, I resisted, as I had seen many surgeons whom I didn't get a good feeling about or didn't trust, and quite frankly, I was doctored out. But when I got in my car to go home, I got a feeling that maybe I should check this doctor out. I called my primary care physician, who coincidentally knew him. She told me she would call him and get back to me. Not long after, I received a call back, and she told me that he was coming in early the next morning to see me. I met with the surgeon the next day, and although we had some differences, when he began to speak, I knew I was in the right place. This one encounter started the ball rolling to a place I had hoped for but saw no way to: a functioning life. He also helped me through other conditions that plagued me as a result of my back problems. My surgeon was there for me personally; he would often call just to check in on me. He traveled the multi-year journey with me, and I always knew that I wasn't in it alone. Without him, I would probably be in a convalescent home somewhere on a morphine drip. He gave me my precious life back.

My spine surgeon was also a true blessing and source of support during my daughter's struggle with her back. When she was fourteen or fifteen, I noticed that her back didn't look straight. I called my doctor, who did me a favor by seeing her, as he does not do pediatrics. Through diagnostic testing, it was disclosed that she had three herniated discs, a spondylolisthesis in the base of her spine, and a disease called Scheurmann's Kyphosis. Her diagnosis was devastating, and we were sent to Boston. Through a very long time of examining her back to see the best way to treat her, she eventually had a spine fusion at only sixteen years of age. Through all the time of diagnostic testing and imaging in Boston and her surgery, my spine surgeon played the role of our consultant. On two occasions, he sat with me in his office and reviewed her imaging pictures that I had brought from Boston to give me his opinion. His input and support throughout that difficult time meant more to my daughter and me than I could ever put into words. The crazy intervention that I received, which I thank the universe that I listened to, not only blessed me but more importantly, my daughter.

Just before I turned fifty, I decided to inquire about going back to school. After not working for many years while I coped with health issues, I knew if I was going to reenter the workforce, I needed to go back to school. Hence, I made an appointment at a local community college just to get more information on their certifications and degrees. After speaking with a woman who explained the programs the college offered, I told her that I would think about it and call her back in a few weeks. She told me that she knew my type and that I would never call her back. She then encouraged me to commit, which I did.

That decision, following the nudge from the advisor, brought me three years of growth and a marked increase in my self-confidence, which I desperately needed. At the onset of my first class, I was terrified because I hadn't been in a classroom for thirty years and didn't have much faith that I would be able to keep up. After my first semester, I was inducted into the Phi Theta Kappa National Honor Society. It was a thrill! When I had started classes, I had heard of PowerPoint but had never used the software. After my first year of classes, I became certified in this Microsoft application. Another thrill! So many wonderful blessings came my way through earning my associate's degree at that community college. My self-confidence increased as I realized that if I applied myself, I could reach amazing heights. I also made lifelong friendships, and I learned that I could write.

In various classes at my college, I had to take the Myers-Briggs Personality Test. This test uses a series of questions to determine your personality traits and what profession(s) best suits you. All five times that I took this test, I received the same answer for the profession that best fit me: a writer. I thought it was a farce because I didn't know how to write, so one professor allowed me to retake it. Once again, there was one profession matched to me: writer. After taking a few classes where I had to write essays, I discovered I actually could write and enjoyed it. I never pursued that field once I began working after graduation. It was a nudge from the universe that took me eleven years to pursue. Better late than never!

A few years ago, I had been thinking about buying a new car, as my Highlander was getting old and failing. I had called a friend to see if she would be available to visit a car dealership with me the next day just to look at the car I wanted, a RAV4. So we made the plans, which I quickly rescinded, feeling like I needed more time to think about it. On my home from work that day, every car that I saw was a RAV4. It was unmistakable that the universe was trying to tell me something. I went with my friend the next day and left the dealership on that exact day with a brand new RAV4. It was a purchase I never regretted.

I had been desiring an Apple Watch. It had been on my "want" list for some time, but without researching, I had assumed that it was too expensive. I had gone to a medical appointment, and the medical assistant who brought me into the examining room was wearing what appeared to be an Apple Watch. When I asked her, she happily took it off and showed me all of the watch's features. She mentioned that it was only twenty dollars more on her cell phone bill to finance it. That was doable for me. The next day, I went to my cell phone provider's store and walked out with my brand new Apple Watch. If I had not met the MA that day and was bold enough to inquire about it, I most likely would still not have the watch that I wanted so badly, and that I love.

When I received the strong nudge of my layoff, perhaps I wasn't listening to the more gentle whispers from the universe about work. The stress and anxiety I was feeling surrounding work had been eating away at me. Although I had tried to transfer, nothing had panned out. I couldn't quit because I am the sole breadwinner in my family. So it seems that my layoff was a sign from the universe to finally remove myself from the toxic environment of my job.

In the fall of 2020, I accepted a job that at first seemed compatible with my desires. But two weeks into my four-week orientation, things took a nasty turn. The environment was difficult and I found myself feeling the emotions that I felt at my previous job. I had decided before I had gone back to work that nothing and nobody would disturb my happiness again. I still had several months of my severance period left as well. I had called a friend and told her that the job was not what I was looking for. I asked her advice if I should resign or stick it out. Her advice was to resign, but I still wasn't sure. When I was driving to my job the next day, all of the streets on my commute were closed, and I kept on getting rerouted. I said out loud as I was driving that it seemed like the universe was rerouting me. When I got to the job, I resigned. And, again, I have never regretted that decision.

When I paid attention to whispers from the universe that were trying to direct me in a certain direction, wonderful things happened. But when I ignored nudges that were presented to me, things didn't turn out as well. One day I picked up my daughter at work. There were two ways that we could have traveled home: the highway or back roads. Something was telling me to go on the back roads, but the highway was a quicker route, so that is the way I went. No sooner had I got on the highway, than I could see bumper-to-bumper traffic ahead. I was lucky to be able to exit the highway before the onset of traffic. Now, when I am out and about driving and get a feeling to go a particular way, I always tune in to that feeling and do what I am told.

One day on a walk with Colby, we hadn't gotten far when Colby started pulling on the leash in the direction toward home, which he had never done before. My first instinct was to encourage him to continue our walk, but instead, I went back in the direction toward home. When we were crossing back onto our road, I noticed that a goose had been hit by a car at the top of my street. As she was painfully trying to move to the side of the road, a gaggle of baby geese waddled their way out from under her and were scattering to safety. I called animal control from my cell phone, and to make a long story short, the mom and two baby geese died, but the animal control officer and I, with the help of a few neighbors, were able to gather up the ten remaining babies to safety. Thankfully, I listened to Colby's intuition and we made it to the scene on time to save those baby geese. If not, they would have been lost forever.

After all of those times being tugged in a certain direction by the universe, and by Colby, I now always listen to those tugs. If I am at a crossroads and feel unsure which direction I should go, I ask the universe to direct me, and I always find that guidance. Ask and ye shall receive!

Now that I am feeling more relaxed and at ease with the voyage I am on, it seems that the smallest of hints that I feel and act on are pushing me further toward the answer of why I was laid off. My travels so far in this period of transition seem to have been led by hints from the universe. I have been more in tune with the universe's subtle, and sometimes not so subtle, hints and nudges. And from my feelings, I know that I am on the right path.

My Italian heritage instilled in me the stubbornness that is a well-known trait of this nationality. And with that stubbornness came a need to be in control. I thought I knew what was best, and I marched to the beat of my own drum even when I met with disaster. Releasing my grip on that control has not been an easy transition for me, but I do feel more like I am swimming with the current rather than fighting it. Life is beginning to not feel so hard. My layoff was a push that has forced me to make changes to weed out what was not working for me. This allowed me to start on a trek to rediscover myself, and it gave me the permission and courage to dream a dream that would not have been possible before this time.

So while my layoff was initially tough, this time was bringing me to an amazing place. My layoff brought me to a better place, similar to how my spine surgeon had. Just as my spine surgeon relieved the stresses from my back, my layoff relieved the stresses of emotional pain that had haunted me throughout my life. I am thankful for this moment, literally this moment, that my soul is calm and full of hope and joy. I am full of excitement for my future.

CHAPTER 13

RELEASING LIMITATIONS

GOING THROUGH THIS TIME AND MOVING FORWARD with new dreams and ambitions, I felt intermittently hindered by those pesky limiting beliefs, thoughts, and feelings. Thoughts of not having enough, not being enough, and doubting my self-worth were periodically weighing me down. After traveling back through time, I realized that these various limitations had been placed on me through life's circumstances and the feelings surrounding my brother's death that I never worked through. I needed to get past these limitations so I could fully embrace the future and my new thirst for growth and advancement.

Through the seven years of my most recent employment, those feelings of not being good enough and feeling held back from my full capacity were always in the back of my mind. In my work and personal life, I took people's opinions of myself too seriously, and I let those opinions dominate my thoughts. I allowed myself to be disrespected and I accepted the value that was placed on me by my superiors as my true worth instead of having the motivation and confidence to set higher goals to move myself ahead. I severely lacked the drive and vigor to believe in myself.

I seemed to always be worried about something—how I was perceived at work, the future and what it held for me. I often found myself worrying about not having enough money. Whenever I spent money on anything other than necessities, I was tormented with guilt. All of these things were robbing me of my happiness. Like attracts like, and I decided that things that made me feel anything but happy had to go. Any time I thought of a negative, I began to replace it with a thought of a positive. Any time a negative image came into my mind, I relied on my visual cues to bring me to my happy place: my golden retriever, the beach, nature, and ice cream, to name a few.

Limiting beliefs were also holding me back. I felt small in every way, small and unworthy of a life worth living. I stagnated without having the capacity to lift myself to be a part of life. Feelings of being invisible that were built into my consciousness through the unfortunate events surrounding Frankie's death were still a part of me. I had never realized that until this time. I accepted that as my reality, as who I was. Feelings of lacking were another constant and recurring thought that plagued me as well.

The feeling that I never had enough time beleaguered me. It was like the same scene in a depressing movie played over and over. Those thoughts of lacking time certainly had brought that into my life. I always felt like a rat on a wheel, running and running and never getting anywhere. I never seemed to have enough time for anything, especially for myself, time to enjoy life. While I didn't realize it earlier, it's not only what we say but what we do and think that bring something into reality.

Constant thoughts of limitations caused those limitations to grow. Repeating and thinking the same things over and over again to myself caused those things to be present in my life. But I didn't have the perspective to see the damage that I was doing. While I originally felt that these limitations were placed on me by others, and while they may have been inspired by others and by outside circumstances, I had allowed them to grow and flourish by giving them the energy of my thoughts. Just as I water my gardens to grow my vegetables and flowers, my consistent watering of limiting and negative beliefs with the energy my thoughts allowed those beliefs to grow to my reality.

I now knew that to live in peace without restrictions, I had to release and detach myself from all the limiting ideas that were blocking my progression. Releasing these limitations allowed me to reassess my life and know that I can be and do anything. I began to have optimism. Releasing limitations gave me the confidence to expand my mind and attract the things I wanted. I learned from some readings that in order to detach and release any negative thoughts and feelings, you must lift them from your subconscious and welcome them without supplying them energy of recognition, while keeping your thoughts only on the present. Sounds a lot easier said than done, right?

The first time I did this, it was overwhelming. Welcoming these detrimental thoughts and feelings was difficult, to put it mildly. But when I felt the negative belief leave me, it was a liberation that I cannot describe. I began with releasing feelings of worry. I invited the worry I felt about losing my job but kept my awareness on the time I was in. I recognized the emotion but did not focus on it. I had to do that a few times, but eventually freeing that worry was like freedom from bondage! I intentionally asked for all of my limiting beliefs and feelings to be brought to my awareness. There were a lot of them! But with patience, and some tears, one by one, I released them. With that release, I felt my mind and self lighten. I felt a freedom that I had never felt before. Freedom from the past led me to freedom in the future.

So, it was now time to say, think, and do what was necessary to turn the life that I was envisioning into my reality. It was now my mission to move forward and live the life I was beginning to view. I now knew what the dominant thoughts in my mind needed to be to bring about my new reality. As thoughts are energy, I needed to shift the energy away from my mind and to awareness.

It was time to start watering my garden with thoughts and beliefs of being limitless, deserving of the life that I had a thirst for. The lessons of meditation made this transition much more accessible. I became my biggest advocate, my biggest cheerleader! The change started within me, from the inside out. Many things inspired this change, none more than the desire for the life that I was feeling would be mine.

CHAPTER 14

WHAT INSPIRED
THE CHANGES THAT BEGAN
TO TURN THINGS AROUND

THE DESIRE FOR LASTING HAPPINESS was the main inspiration behind my changes. My life up until this point had happy times, but those times were darkened by negative ideas, emotions, and feelings that seemed to be a part of me. I wanted to free myself from the stresses of life and expand myself and my mind to continue to feel worthy of the life I was aspiring to. It was time to be joyful with all that my life contained.

I knew I did not want to revisit the state of my life prior to my layoff. I no longer wanted to feel small. I had seen the enormity of the world and had developed a thirst to be a part of it. I needed to create goals and dreams that would keep me reaching for the stars. After this time of reflection, I knew that the way I felt as I climbed the mountain to find happiness and freedom from my mind was what encouraged me to keep on ascending.

After some reading that I had done, I was moved to reflect on my energy through this earthly time. I no longer wanted to see my time here as being like a ball of elastics, wound up so tight that I couldn't move past the bondage of my negative thoughts and feelings. I wanted to see myself as confident, someone who reached for whatever she wanted with no apprehension. I wanted my time here to be happy and successful, with a success measured by my standards. I mostly wanted to see myself as living my absolute best life.

It was time for me to create the vision that would support how I wanted to view my energy here. I saw myself chasing a vision that I witnessed through my dad.

My dad had a vision for himself and his family, and he worked every day to create that vision. My ambitious father was always growing, personally and with the business. He was involved in town and state politics, and eventually he got his real estate license. While he didn't let anything stop him from creating his vision, he was always kind and treated everyone that he met along the way with respect. He pursued goals that provided him growth. Because of his determination for advancement, we had a wonderful life. We never lacked. He died at the age of eighty-three. At the time, he was still working every day, even Saturdays. No matter his age, he still toiled toward his vision.

I somehow lost that in myself, but not anymore! A new kid was in town, and it was time for that sixty-year-old kid to design the vision of a life that she now desired and felt worthy of. It was time to begin the next chapter of the life that I was beginning to dream of. It was both physical, the things that I wanted, and emotional, how I wanted to feel. It was time for creation!

CHAPTER 15

WHAT DO I WANT?

ONCE I SHIFTED MY FOCUS TO WHAT I WANTED, it was time to create my future from lessons from the past. Disconnecting from the past provided me permission to dream about the future. For the first time in my life, I could design the life I wanted. With the world as my catalog, it was time to place my order.

I sat myself down one day to create a list of what I wanted. My efforts started slow, but I soon began to use a spotlight on my catalog rather than a nightlight. While at first it felt a little self-absorbed, I quickly realized it wasn't. It was ambition. It was the aspiration for a better life.

This process was life changing, literally. I was ordering my life, what I wanted that would make me feel fulfilled and bring me closer to my vision. I was forging ahead with this practice and choosing what I wanted, big or small. It took quite some time, but I eventually had three hundred things on my list. Whaat?? I didn't know how I would attain many of these things, but I put them on my list no matter what. I granted myself permission to fantasize, as well as permission to ask the universe to guide me.

The act of creating my list increased my feelings of a positive, full life. I was seeing these dreams with trust and faith in the universe. I knew what I wanted, and I now I had to focus on those desires. My order to the universe brought with it a feeling of confidence and excitement that I never felt before. This list was my road map, but I kept my focus on growth to those desires. If I began to feel any doubt, I released that doubt. Whenever I felt any limitations coming back to my mind, I gave no focus to those feelings and instead kept in my thoughts an image of something I wanted. I began seeing myself as the owner of this new life that I had ordered.

To micromanage my list, I created a list of ten items that I most wanted. And I wrote how I would feel when I received these items. I tucked this list in my pocket and it came along with me as I traveled through my day. Any free time that I found throughout my day, even waiting for a doctor's appointment, I would read my list, and after reading each desire, I said thank you. This practice made me feel like I already had it. The manifesting of what I wanted was no longer a chance; I owned it and felt like it was already mine.

I dreamed big! Go big or go home, right? My thoughts of what I wanted certainly started small. But as my mind expanded, and as I gave myself more permission to dream, thoughts just overflowed. I went from feeling so small to now feeling deserving of what I wanted. My list included everything from the amount of money I wanted, experiences that I wanted to enjoy, what I wanted professionally, my health and body (which I am pretty secure about save a few things), material things I wanted, and places that I wanted to go. My list grew and grew!

During this time of daring to dream, there were a few moments of uncertainty, but having this list became the road map to my existence. With these new revelations, I decided to create a vision board. Through local social media pages I belong to, I created a post asking if anybody had any old magazines. I managed to collect a vast variety and amount of magazines. I went through dozens and dozens of magazines looking for images and words that represented as much on my list as possible. My vision board, which I placed on a wall by my bed, gave me something concrete to look at and focus on. It was a direct route from my eyes, to my thoughts, and to my life. I became focused on my vision, and this would define my life. It was exhilarating! My small footprint on life began to wane as my thoughts broadened.

Growth flourishes where your attention is focused. And my life began to grow. But it wasn't growing with only things; faith in myself was growing as well. I seemed to ease through my life, whereas not that far in the past, life felt hard. I got frustrated, annoyed, and upset much less frequently than before. I was developing the attitude and mindset that began to match my vision.

Determining exactly what I wanted and having the confidence, determination, and drive to chase these desires was a turning point for me, as it allowed me to accept my past. I now am thankful for all of my experiences, the good ones and the hard ones equally. It is those experiences that have taught me what I want and don't want. This wisdom guides me in my growth.

CHAPTER 16

GROWTH AND ADVANCEMENT

I HAD LOST THE DESIRE FOR GROWTH SOMEHOW in the previous eight years. Once I started to focus on what I wanted, I began to see and feel the cultivation of the seeds I had planted through defining my desires. During this time that I was able to spread my wings and expand my reality, I began to feel a sense of ease while releasing the energy that was holding me back. My confidence grew with gusto for the life I was beginning to grasp hold of. The more I felt myself moving in the direction of my dreams, the more I felt confirmation from life that I was moving in the right direction. The exhilaration that I was feeling confirmed that I was heading in the right direction.

I continued to place myself in situations and places where I felt inspired. The beach where we spent time last summer is located in an area of extreme wealth. For example, Taylor Swift has a summer home a half-mile from the beach that we go to. Placing myself in this area brought thoughts and feelings of prosperity and wealth, and what I was feeling, I was absorbing. It was the natural abundance of the ocean, but it was also the feeling of success in the area that provided inspiration and guidance to chase my dreams. I had often felt very insignificant, but those feelings were no longer a part of me as my field of energy felt empowered.

Along with the beach, one of the special places I love to go is the West Hartford Reservoir. It is special because my brother Frankie and I used to spend time there together. Frankie certainly lived life to the fullest. He lived such a big life, accomplishing so much before the age of sixteen. His zest for a full life inspires the same for me as I recall the memories of us during our time at the reservoir. It does make me wonder if he somehow knew that his life was going to be short. Fifty years later, it is still a favorite place to visit. Whether it's just Colby and me, or whether a friend or my daughter joins us, it is a place where I always feel good. Being in a place that bridges happy memories and inspiration from the past to the inspired person who was now living through the example of her departed brother was extraordinary. Now whenever I am at this special place, I can feel my brother cheering me on.

Focusing not only on what I wanted but how I wanted to feel allowed growth. The desire for growth and advancement kept me moving forward and provided me with growing self-confidence that I could achieve what I wanted, could be who I wanted, and could do what I wanted. I was feeling and seeing more of the "why" for my layoff: to find the person who was lost inside of me.

I also had to protect my energy through this time. Anything that made me feel less than positive and limitless had to be removed. To maintain my newly found sense of growth, I had to surround myself with the environment and people who supported my efforts through their words and energy. So it was time to do some energy cleaning.

My daughter, who lives with me, had an occasional tendency to be negative. I sat down with her one day and told her that when she was home, the negativity had to stop. It took a little practice, but she no longer is negative at home. I have a friend who also has an intermittent tendency to be negative. When she would come over, there often was a lot of complaining. I eventually told her that when she was around me, the complaining had to stop. We were only going to talk about positive things. As did my daughter, my friend began to respect my efforts to have a positive mind and life. My mother's words (and those of many mothers, I am sure), "If you don't have anything nice to say, don't say anything at all," were very wise advice. A positive mind equals a positive life.

I also had to stop watching the news. The majority of news coverage is stressful, especially throughout the pandemic. I kept up to date with my local news as the pandemic unfolded, but that was it. Cutting down on news also cut down on another topic that is stressful to me—politics. Limiting my exposure to news channels was one of my best decisions ever!

Protecting my energy and setting boundaries was paramount to maintaining my happiness. As well, searching for my passions and purpose in life would guide me to my dreams and goals that would support and sustain my contentment. Taking time to explore what I am here to do would give meaning to my life. It was time to search within to delineate these important questions.

CHAPTER 17

FINDING MY PASSIONS
AND PURPOSE

I WAS ASKED BY A SUCCESS COACH IN THE FALL OF 2020 what my passions and purpose were. I couldn't respond; I had no idea. At the age of sixty, I had never given thought to define my passions and purpose. I had lost what made me happy, what I wanted to be known for, and how I wanted to make my mark on the world. I lost focus on myself. And, while we have responsibilities in our daily lives, the person who we should be most accountable to is ourself. To keep myself, my dreams, and my goals at the forefront, I had to discover my passions and purpose because they would guide me to those desires that would make my life meaningful.

To determine my passions and purpose, I began to dig deeper into myself. When I was in school earning my associate's degree, the growth from learning changed things for me. But this time, where I was digging deeper to truly discover Sally was what would identify and define the direction that I would focus my attention. It was time to grow into myself; it was time to answer this important question: What are my passions? What makes my heart sing? What makes my life bright? What do I love to do most in the world? What could I spend my whole day doing? What makes me completely happy and brings endless joy and fulfillment? What shapes and forms my personality? The answers to these questions would bring me closer to defining my passions.

I love to cook. Cooking is something that I have happily spent a whole day doing. I am like my mother in that way. My mother would spend all day cooking for her family. It was a symbolic gesture of love for her family and friends. She made epic Sunday dinners that always included family and often friends and neighbors. On Christmas Eve, she cooked for several days to prepare the feast of the seven fishes, an Italian tradition. I love to cook for the same reasons, for the love of my family, friends, and myself. I love spending a day on the weekend just cooking. Having a few things in the freezer that I can quickly thaw for dinner is a big help for busy weekdays. I was thrilled when I was finally able to cook by myself, including chopping the veggies, to make a big pot of turkey chili after my shoulder surgery recovery. And it's not only cooking, but baking is right up there as well.

While my mom only baked on one holiday, I love to bake all year round. My mom was not a big baker, except on Good Friday. Every Good Friday my family and I looked forward to waking up to the smell of freshly baking homemade bread. My mom baked not only for us, but for what seemed like half the town. She used to make traditional Italian Easter bread, where she weaved the bread dough around colored hard-boiled eggs. It was such a treat! I spent what often seemed like an entire day delivering bread to all of her friends in town. Many people looked forward to Good Friday, not just my family.

My baking didn't include bread unless it came from a bread maker—not exactly homemade bread, but delicious nonetheless. I love baking for family and friends equally. I am also big on traditions. Ever since I was sixteen, I did all the holiday baking for my family, which I loved! Pizzelles are a popular Italian cookie and a tradition in my family going back for as long as I can remember. My daughter and I are the only ones in my immediate family who have carried on this tradition. Right after Thanksgiving my daughter and I make a double batch of these delicious cookies, which takes several hours. We eat some, but most are given to family, friends, and neighbors. This year I even shipped some to a cousin in Florida. A friend, my daughter, my friend's son, and I have an annual marathon holiday baking day just before Christmas. We start early in the morning, and most often our last batch comes out of the oven at 10:00 P.M. While most go to the same group of family, friends, and neighbors, we do make sure to taste a few just to make sure they are worthy to share.

I also get much enjoyment out of baking treats for my golden retriever. My daughter and I enjoy baking Colby a birthday cake every year on his birthday. His tail wags as we sing to him and as he gets his first lick of the frosting. Although he doesn't know that we made them for him, Colby's enjoyment in eating the treats makes the effort so worth it. And I love knowing what he's eating. Often, I share the dog treats that I have baked with friends' dogs. So, yes, the joy I get from cooking and baking certainly defines these acts of love as a passion.

Colby, my sweet golden who you are all familiar with at this point, is a special passion of mine. I didn't realize until after Kylie died that she balanced me, and now Colby has taken that responsibility. When I get home, I know that he will be waiting for me with exuberant enthusiasm to greet me. There's nothing quite like being so loved!! I am thankful for my Colby, and for the dog that I lost. Dogs are nonjudgmental and are the absolute best at keeping secrets. He is always happy to be with me, as I am to be with him. All seems right with the world when I feel him lying on my feet at night. I think he gets just as much peace when I am petting and stroking his fur as he gives me. He doesn't care what my hair looks like, or if I have makeup on, he loves me and accepts me for me. And he keeps me fit with all of the walks and hikes we do. Dogs also seem to have a special way of making their owners more social. With Colby, thanks to his breeder, we have been connected with his siblings and other family members of his who have become wonderful friends whom we see often. In every way, Colby is a passion!

Hiking is a passion, as it places me surrounded by nature. It combines two passions into one because Colby always joins me on hiking expeditions. It is also an awesome cardio workout. As I have mentioned previously, hiking makes me feel connected with abundance. One can't help but be inspired when they are in the middle of the vastness of nature. It is a beautiful thing. Hiking nourishes my body through exercise. Our hiking adventures always include socializing, as we are stopped by countless people who ask if they can say hi to my little man. It makes my heart sing when strangers recognize and appreciate my little buddy's amazing personality. We go hiking often, as it is a favorite way to spend time.

Family is a passion. I have a very large extended family. My mom was from a family of seven, and my dad from a family of ten. I stay connected with my long-distance family as much as possible. My immediate family is strained, and I have one child, my daughter. One of the biggest gifts of this time has been the opportunity to reestablish my and Erica's relationship. We both were always so busy with our lives that we lost touch with each other. Whether going out to dinner, or shopping, or just spending time together watching a movie, this time has been an important opportunity for us to reconnect. This past year brought my daughter and I together in a wonderful and meaningful way.

Meditation has become a surprise passion of mine. I always thought meditation was kind of a weird thing. But as I mentioned earlier, this pause in time nudged me to give it a try. It has now become a morning ritual and I can't start any day without it. I have discovered a gratitude meditation on a streaming service that has become a staple for me. Gratitude and meditation have become the cornerstones of my life. They keep me focused on what's most important, staying mindful of my blessings. They also keep me present, enjoying the time I am in while feeling thankful for everything that I have. As is a house, we are nothing without a strong foundation, and meditation and gratitude are the foundation for all that I do and feel.

Fun is one of my greatest passions. I had lost my zest for fun, but it is now essential to me. Having fun lightens me and brings out my personality. When I am out and about doing something that brings me joy and excitement, it is a release from everyday responsibilities. All worries are left behind. The beach certainly brought endless fun and happiness to me and my family and friends last year. Having fun energizes me, and I make sure that every day includes something that brings out a kid-like quality in me. Enjoying time with friends is important for my social life. Maintaining friendships with people who are supportive and accepting of all that I represent is of the utmost importance for me. And I can always count on Colby for a laugh or two. For me, fun is not a luxury, it is a necessity.

And my absolute greatest passion is writing. Writing calms my mind and gives voice to my true self; it expresses who I am. It allows me to convey my thoughts in a meaningful, thoughtful way. Writing allows me to be creative. When I am in the process of writing, I forget all about time and lose myself in my thoughts. I have to set a timer when I am writing, or else I will look at the clock and three hours will have flown by. Writing gives me time to reflect on my thoughts and to think about how I want to say something without just blurting it out. I am able to carefully choose what I want to say and be more descriptive of my true feelings through those words. This form of communication gives me confidence in my voice, my inner voice. It allows something to be uncovered about myself, without exposing myself outwardly. I am baring myself and my thoughts through my words. Writing helped me to find my voice and allows me to be my authentic self.

It seems, having defined my passions, that a passion is something that does not have a defined time. When I am doing anything that I consider a passion, I am not watching the clock. When I am connected with the people or experience without thoughts of anything further, I can appreciate and get more out of the experience.

I have found over the last several months as I have been traveling on this voyage that not having a defined purpose left me aimless. My purpose is the foundation on which my passions are built. My purpose is the reason why I am doing what I am doing. Defining my passions gave me direction to my purpose.

Now, to define my purpose. My purpose is what completes me. It shapes and forms my identity. It is what I put my time and energy into that fulfills me. My purpose is the impact that I want to make on the world, and the deep reason for my being. It is my foundation. When I type those words, there is one thought that comes to my mind: to inspire. Yes, my purpose is to inspire those around me, those who are on their way to me, and those whom I will never meet.

Through this book, I hope to spark inspiration in those who can relate to something in my past or through this time. One of the hardest lessons I have learned throughout the writing of this book is how feelings, if not worked out, get buried in your subconscious and stay there until you let them go. If nothing else, It is my hope that something in my words will help someone who has had an event in their life that left negative, limiting feelings. That is probably all of us to some capacity.

I hope for people who, like myself, feel like they don't have a spot in the world, who feel small within their own shadow or the shadow of others. I hope that somewhere within my writings they find themselves, their voice, or their place. I am now standing tall, confident, and bright within myself. The reason for writing this book was to share my story and my journey. But in the process, I have learned so much about myself. I hope to inspire those who need a spark to find their true self, or whatever else they may be searching for.

Through the person that I have now found, I hope to inspire my daughter to stand bright in her own life. My wish is that she never lets any circumstance or person make her feel less than the amazing person that she is. I hope this book inspires her to always reach for the stars and to never stop growing. My wish is that she will find her voice, find what makes her heart sing, follow the music that inspires her, and close the door to anything that disrupts her happiness. To my daughter: I hope I am inspiring you through my journey to the person I have found, that you stay bright, work toward your goals, and stay true to the beautiful person that you are.

Last fall when I was collecting magazines for my vision board, one man messaged me that he had some magazines that I could have. He proceeded to ask me what I would be using the magazines for. When I told him that I would be using them to create a vision board, he told me that I was inspiring him to do the same. Once I had gone through his magazines, I returned them to him, along with others I had collected, and a few of my own. He was grateful and later told me that he had made his first vision board. It felt so wonderful to have inspired him!

It is my hope in the future to start a nonprofit organization. I already have a name for my organization but will hold that to myself for now. Once my book is complete and published, I want to help people who are desiring to make a change like myself by donating copies of my book, as well as books and programs that have assisted me on my travels through this time. I hope to inspire others to find their light who may now be shadowed, just as I found mine through the books and words of others who helped me to find my place in the world.

I hope I inspire others to continue to chase rainbows that will lead to their pot of gold. I learned the hard way that not having goals and dreams to aspire to left me traveling through life feeling lost. The other day when I was driving around doing errands, I realized for the first time, at the age of sixty, that I knew what I wanted to be and where I wanted to go. That thought brought such a feeling of elation that I felt I was going to burst. That feeling is what I hope for all, the feeling of loving life. That is my purpose, to inspire others to be, feel, and do what strikes a chord within your heart and soul!

CHAPTER 18

DEFINING MY OWN DESTINY

THE GIFT OF TIME GIVEN BY MY LAYOFF brought the opportunity to lift myself to new heights and be a part of the universe instead of standing on the sidelines. I began to shift my paradigm from focusing on the heaviness of each day to focusing on how light I felt and the ease in which I moved. The path that I am now traveling is leading me toward the direction of my desires. For me to make this trek, I had to rid myself of my past habits of feeling like I was swallowed up by the universe's power. To move forward, I had to unburden my mind of negative thoughts so I could move forward to the vision I had created.

I needed to identify past habits that had brought me to this place and learn from them so I would be able to continue my growth and not allow myself to get lost again. At the lovely age of sixty, and I mean that sincerely, I examined my life's journey and found what was working and what no longer served me well. I defined what I wanted and didn't want. By changing my daily way of doing things, starting with gratitude, I began to move in a better direction.

I sat down with an open mind of being and feeling limitless to determine what I wanted in my life, knowing that I would never allow anyone to ever make me feel less than my true self. I will never surround myself with people who will shake my faith. I am a new person through this time with the inner strength to go for it!

I define my destiny not solely based on what I want to have and experience but also on what I want to feel. I desire more life. I want to feel strong and unstoppable on the inside while displaying confidence through my actions on the outside.

I have changed and have taken back control of my destiny. I am on the path of greatness, happiness, and fulfillment. I will keep on readjusting as necessary to reach and achieve all of my dreams. I have taken control of my path through life instead of allowing fate to control my direction. Life no longer happens to me, life happens for me. My destiny, my journey through my time here, should be happy, and now it is.

I am the architect of my future. While I once relied on fate to guide me, I am now freed from that dependency. I am liberated of being terrified of what was going to happen next, the fear that if too much good was happening, something bad was close by. Not anymore.

Part of erecting the life that I want was creating a list of what I wanted to attain. Having my list helped to focus my mind on what I wanted, thereby deleting from my mind what I didn't want. But my list was just an outline. What would motivate me, not just to write down my desires, but to bring those aspirations into my life? The answer was goals.

CHAPTER 19

CREATING GOALS

Because of my prior lack of direction—okay, no direction—and just going along with life with no focus on my destiny, I had never written goals. I never really thought of the big picture, what I wanted while traveling through this life. I had no thought of ever reaching for anything that seemed beyond my grasp. My mind was so small. Fast forward to 2021!!

Through this period of discovery, I now realize how important goals are. They guide me toward what I want. The ambitions that I identify will lead me to the destination that I chose for myself. I began to feel deserving of not only a bigger life but more life. The list of what I wanted was big, and it was the confidence and feeling like I was deserving of that bigger life that allowed me to dream. But I could not rely only on the list I created. Written-out goals created a measurable way to view my success.

My desires were not my goals, but my goals were drawn from my desires. Goal setting kept me moving in the direction of my dreams. It is not only the actual target that is my focus, it is also how I will feel when I achieve my targeted desire. It is the WHY—why I desire a particular element. And how that accomplishment is going to make me feel when I achieve it. Desires are thoughts emphasized by emotion. Goals represent a time frame for my desires.

Setting goals meant that I was not relying on fate to manifest my desires in my life. Having goals for my desires put me back in the driver's seat. They gave me a sense of accomplishment. It is odd that at work I had daily, weekly, and monthly goals but no personal aims. Why didn't I have this same dedication to progress in my regular life? Because I put everyone and everything ahead of myself. But that has changed.

My newly discovered sense of self allowed me to focus on my own ambitions. The desire to dream big, to order what I wanted from the vast catalog of the universe, helped me to zero in on my direction. Writing out my goals instead of just trying to remember them (the sixty-year-old memory is not what it used to be) keeps me accountable. My targeted desires are written in the present tense: I am so happy and grateful now that I have _____. I am so happy and grateful now that I have accomplished _____. Having my desires written in the present tense makes me feel like I have already achieved them. It places me in the mindset of expectance, not chance. I live in the moment, staying in control of my desires and having faith in my journey to direct me.

While my goals gave me a destination of where I wanted to be and what I wanted to have, creating smaller steps to attain those larger goals was key for me. One of my yearly goals was to write a book. Any time prior to now, I would never have dreamed I could write a book. But I wrote down smaller goals to get me to the big one. Some of the steps to writing this book included writing an outline and committing to writing five thousand words a week. Completing all of these smaller goals made me feel successful, and

I celebrated each one. It was all of the small ambitions that helped me accomplish the big goal. I kept my eye on the prize!

Having my goals keeps the momentum of growth expanding, to keep moving forward. Goals remind me every day where I am going, so that I keep moving forward and not slipping back They are keeping me in check and giving me a clear and precise road map to maintaining my growth.

My daily goals include keeping positive and staying in control of my thoughts. I make the conscious effort to not let any negativity get into my head that will disrupt my peace. My goals helped me determine what I want to achieve in my life, not what my limited mind wanted but what my unlimited self wanted. Whether they are daily, weekly, monthly, or yearly aspirations, I have developed faith in and worthiness of my preset goals, and I maintain faith every day that I will bring what I want to my life. Besides goals, setting intentions also became a useful tool to map out my day and beyond.

CHAPTER 20

SETTING INTENTIONS

SETTING INTENTIONS HAS CHANGED THE WAY I enter into a day or an event as my day progresses. Intentions allow me to set the wheels in motion for a specific outcome that I desire. Whether set at the beginning of the year, day, or a certain activity, intentions send a message to the universe that this is what I am going to do and this is how it's going to go. For me, stating intentions is like sending out positive vibes; it takes the guesswork out of my day and allows for all to go well. Intentions make me the developmental director of my day and life. Whether stated aloud or to myself, they are thoughts directed toward a desired outcome.

Could it be that my layoff was the universe's way to set an intention to guide me to a positive life? I am taking the universe's lead to set intentions to support my new direction. This direction is keeping me mindful and keeping the journey positive with directives that I can transmit out to the airwaves of cosmic energy.

When I wake up in the morning, before even setting my feet on the floor, I go over my day in my mind and set directives for the day. Just like planning ahead for an event, setting intentions helps me plan ahead for the outcome which I desire. After each intent, I set a directive for a magnificent outcome. It is a general road map that makes me feel ready for the day. I no longer feel like I am going into any part of my day blindly.

Setting intentions shows how powerful and influential I am. It is exhilarating that I can shape the day according to a statement displaying intent. I can predetermine my day and all that the day holds. It is another way that I no longer feel like a product of circumstance.

I put out in the world that which I intend to attract from the world through intentions. When I view the world, I focus on being connected with the abundance of everything that I observe and experience. I am not just at the beach, I am a part of the abundance of beach, I am connected to the bounty of the universe through the beach.

As intentions keep my thoughts directed toward the desired outcome I wish for my life, exercise sets the intention to my body for the desired outcome of good health. Exercise and fitness are an important part of my life. Being active keeps my body and spirit flowing in the direction that I choose. I am making an intentional decision to take care of my body to lead it to a place that I wish it to be. When I was sedentary throughout my back challenges, that nonactive lifestyle did much damage to my body. I developed osteoporosis in my late thirties, most likely from being nonfunctional and sedentary. I also developed several conditions because of the odd movement of my body, unknowingly favoring one particular side of my body because of the amount of pain I was in. I wore out my sacroiliac joint, and the right side of my pelvis had rotated out of the joint. So I know the outcome of being inactive, and now I make the intentional choice to be active to hopefully maintain mobility and health as I age.

As I intentionally retained the hope for a better life when I struggled with my back, I set the wheels in motion for a life free of chronic, debilitating pain. While I rarely speak of those difficult times, their lessons are significant. That time could have consumed me, which chronic pain often often did. But for some reason, I never lost the vision of a better, healthier life. Just as my faith was strong as I set intentions for a greater life throughout my health struggles, my faith and intentions are strong now for the life that I keep in my vision.

The intentions to have a joyful life that my goals and dreams will bring to me have been set in motion. I live with faith and expectations of this life. While I am in the process of bringing my vision to fruition, my deliberate and intentional thoughts are that I already am living my vision. And I truly am just by writing this book.

Whether it is the beach, grocery store, or anywhere that I am off to, I set an intention for a close parking space, or a specific space. The area of our favorite beach in Rhode Island is very crowded and it is often hard to find a parking space. Ever since I have become familiar with setting intentions, I always envision a specific parking space that is right in front of the ice cream stand (no surprise) being open and available when we arrive. And every single time we arrive at the beach, that space is waiting for me. For me, this is proof positive of the power of intentions.

The first time I sat down to write this book, I set the intent that thoughts and ideas would flood my mind regarding the content and structure of my book. All went well that first day, and a feeling of accomplishment consumed me. The next day I sat down to write, and things weren't as productive as the first day. How could my first day have gone so well and the second day of writing be such a letdown? Later on that day, I realized that I forgot to set those same intentions as I did on my first day. I can promise you that I never made that mistake again.

Now, no matter what I am doing or plan to do, I set intentions. And, throughout my day, I set intentions for how I wish for things to go for the individual things, small or large, that I find myself doing as my day progresses. Whether it be envisioning no traffic along my journey, finding close parking spaces, finding everything I need while shopping, or arriving home safely, intentions are a handy tool that I use every day. While intentions send out positive vibes for a specific outcome I am envisioning, affirmations, when repeated often, set the tone for making positive changes.

CHAPTER 21

POSITIVE AFFIRMATIONS

POSITIVE AFFIRMATIONS ARE ALWAYS WRITTEN in the present tense so they are already one's reality. They are positive statements that help to challenge and overcome self-sabotaging and negative thoughts. They can help to turn all negatives into positives. Just replacing any phrase that begins with "I can't" with "I can" makes that switch for me. These positive statements keep my mind in sync with my new reality.

Getting into the habit of stating positive affirmations, or mantras, to myself began to program my mind for success. Stating to myself that I can be what I want to be removes the limitations that I once allowed others to place on me. Keeping my thoughts on being limitless changed my awareness of myself to these new feelings. I began to feed into my mind what I now knew to be true: that I am capable of anything that I want to be, have, or feel.

One of my favorite daily mantras is "I am whole, perfect, strong, powerful, loving, harmonious, and happy." I saw this statement somewhere quite some time ago, and it stuck to my memory. I used to repeat it a few years ago, but I never really felt the words to be true, so I stopped. Now, when I voice these words, I feel and believe all that I am saying. I repeat this statement multiple times a day and it keeps me in harmony with my vision.

These positive statements helped to unlock the law of attraction and began to create the life that I knew to be mine. At the beginning of this year, 2021, I was tossing around the idea of writing a book. I had no idea how to write a book, but the thought stayed with me. When I wrote my goals for this year, the top goal was to write a book. I got up one morning and stated, "I am going to write a book." I generally had an idea of what I was going to write about but knew nothing beyond that. The same morning, I was on a website and found an e-book about writing your first book, which I downloaded immediately. I began reading it that day and followed all the steps that guided me through the process to where I am today. I wouldn't have had the confidence or drive to do this previous to this time.

When my manuscript for this book had gone through many personal edits, I knew it was time to find an actual editor. Given this was my first need for an editor, I had no idea how to go about this important step for the progression of my manuscript to an eventual book. One morning I stated, "I am going to be directed to the editor who will embrace my vision of my book and work with me to bring my vision to life." Something led me to a writer's group on Facebook that I am a member of, and there was a recent post on how to find an editor. I searched using that information and my editor was one name that was generated from my search. I checked a few editors' websites, but something attracted me to one particular editor. Within an hour, I messaged the editor, she messaged me back, and we got the ball rolling that day. That person is the wonderful editor who helped to convert my manuscript to this book.

Positive affirmations reprogrammed my mind for success and achievement. They changed the fears and doubts to certainty.

This new habit of putting a focus on daily mantras created positive changes and boosted my self-esteem. My feeling of lack was turned around. Positive affirmations emphasize my happiness and make me a priority.

Along with gratitude, refocusing my feelings and beliefs on positivity is the foundation to receiving the things I want. I have refocused on my new confident self, which has allowed me to set my sights high and to feel unlimited. I fed my mind with mantras that made me hold my head higher and feel taller, and that broadened and brightened my outlook on life. My initial focus, and many in between, didn't work out, so I took another shot. With all the filters removed, this shot changed me on the inside, and those changes began to reflect how the universe and I perceived me.

Along with "I am whole, perfect, strong, powerful, loving, harmonious, and happy," some of my favorite affirmations that I am in the habit of saying multiple times a day are the following: "I am a powerful magnet for wealth, money, prosperity, abundance, good health, and love." "I am unlimited." "Only good can come into my life." "Life is so easy, life is so good, all good things come to me." "I am financially free." Through these statements, I created a person whom the universe perceived to be open and confident and ready to accept those things into my life that I had set my affirmations for.

I also put out to the universe positive affirmations and thoughts for a new job. Even though I had the safety net of my severance package, feelings of uneasiness still crept in about not having an actual job. I recognized uneasiness to be a negative emotion and released it so I would not attract other things in my life that would cause uneasy feelings (I am learning). Such a powerful exercise! I often say, "A better job with more money is on its way to me." With this mantra, I continually have faith that the universe will direct me to the right position, or direct it to me. Through all of this time, I have kept a schedule as though I am working. While writing my book, I have treated this as my job. I created a writing schedule as I would have created a regular work schedule. I set my alarm to the same time as for my previous job. I make my lunch the night before, just as I did when I worked outside of my home. My positive affirmations, attitude, and habits will somehow attract the perfect position that is meant for me. I have absolute faith in that.

It was not only positive affirmations that were changing me, it was my confidence, doing things in a certain way, focusing on my passions and purpose, that brought me in unity with the universe. Before this time, and even now, balance sometimes seems off. Focusing on a balance that I could establish and maintain so I did not revert to my old self is another element paramount to the success of my future.

CHAPTER 22

CREATING BALANCE

THERE WERE SO MANY SIGNS that my balance in life was off, but I did not have the tools I needed, or time, it seemed, to make changes. My to-do list was outrageously long but never seemed to include time for me. All my thoughts and lists of things to do were about what groceries I needed and what errands needed to be run. I was really busy but too out of sync with my existence to make changes. I was always exhausted at the end of the day, and although I was productive at completing my to-do lists, I was unproductive at nurturing my energy and my life. Life was zipping past, but my flow of energy was sluggish. Throughout this voyage, I have been shown in so many ways how my layoff was a gift. I have been able to refocus on myself and begin the rebirth of my life. Now it was time to find my balance.

Creating a balance between my passions and purpose made life worthwhile and a joy, more joy than I could ever remember. I always kept in mind my passions, what made my heart sing, and my newly defined purpose, my reason for being on this earth. I was put on this earth to inspire. I have found my voice through writing. My passions—cooking, baking, Colby/dogs, hiking, spending time with family and friends, meditation, beach time, having fun, and writing—were wonderful and often aligned with my purpose. My passions brought fun and happiness to my life, while my purpose brought meaning to my life. Symmetry of my passions and purpose makes my life balanced and meaningful.

Scheduling time just for me was the start of tipping the scale in my favor. Every day I took time just for me. Often, it was reading for pleasure, or simply looking at a magazine. It was an escape to relish my peace and enjoy being able to take time and care for myself, without feeling guilty over all the things I should be doing.

In that balance was also applying for jobs. I often obsessed over waiting for my phone to ring in response to applications that I had submitted. I soon realized that I had to apply and let it go and that the right position would come to me. Like my life now, I had to be mindful to not obsess over any particular thing. I put my intentions out to the universe through applying for jobs, and then placed my faith in the universe that the right position would find its way to me. That was all I could do.

I became more aware of how I was spending my time and feeling the balance with what I did. The most important part of the balance was of my mind and self. I had lost that part of me, and recovering that balance through this journey of discovery was of the utmost importance. People were starting to become aware of the change in my energy. I began feeling centered to my core, finally feeling balance with the universe, a distinct feeling that life was becoming easier and less complicated. I made sure that I was not consumed by any particular thing. Most importantly, all was done calmly. Gratitude brought me in harmony with the universe. I felt gratitude for the new day, gratitude for my life, and all that my life comprised. I was being sure that I was in harmony with what I did, and that those things brought happiness and fun to my life. I found myself enjoying getting up early so I didn't waste any of my gift of time to renew my being. Every moment that I was awake was a chance for growth, a chance to enjoy my life, and a chance to be present and aware of all of the changes that were uncovering the person who was coming into herself.

I was developing a balance within my body. I made sure that I was feeding my body well, usually. And, to balance my obsession for ice cream, I was conscientious to exercise to offset the extra calories. I do believe my sole purpose for exercising last summer was to support my obsession for this delicious frozen treat. And this obsession created a balance of family time, which was important for the balance of my life.

This pause of time in my life brought awareness of my family. Family time became an important component of the stability of my life. While we spent much time in search of the best ice cream, It wasn't just the ice cream that was important, it was being out as a family and being present to enjoy our time together. No matter what we were doing, we always had fun. Fun had been missing from my life, and I realized the importance of letting go of all the responsibilities of being an adult, once in a while. I permitted myself to experience the enjoyment of being free and seeing life through the eyes of a child. When we were out as a family, time was nonexistent. The only concern was family, free and clear from any other thoughts. It was fabulous! Once I understood that life is a journey and not a destination to my grave, the freeness of my mind grew. I allowed myself to enjoy the entire ride instead of always being concerned about where I was going. As with my goals, I placed just as much importance on enjoying my way to my desire as I did of attaining that desire. I always seemed to have so much to do, and my only thoughts were on what I had to get done. But life is about enjoying the journey without being so focused on the journey's end.

My balance in all ways became intentional mindfulness of my thoughts and actions, to make sure that all that was important to me, all that kept my mind at peace, all that gave my life purpose was in sync. When I was writing my book, I set a timer on my watch in twenty-five-minute segments, so I was not only focused on writing but also being sure that I wasn't ignoring those around me, such as my golden retriever, who almost always was asleep on my feet. I wrote for twenty-five minutes and took five minutes off until I had written the number of words I had committed to writing per day. Keeping current with friends and regularly scheduling time to spend with them was also part of the symmetry, as was special one-on-one time with my daughter, my dog, and all of us together as a family unit.

Equilibrium at this time also includes my mental health. I have never had the tools that I have now since I became aware of the activity and energy of thoughts. I do my best to not energize the running ticker of comments in my mind with the attention of thought. It is the balance of keeping my emotions and feelings in check that makes me feel like a completely different person than I used to be.

I have become acutely aware of the signs of not being balanced—in my feelings and thoughts and also in how my time was spent. The way I spend my time is a conscious and constant effort that includes my daily routine and staying connected with friends. I also welcome new challenges to my life. I never say no to trying something new. All of these new things welcome and define growth. I make sure, subconsciously, to keep a mental checklist to ensure that my time spent was purposeful.

The goals and vision I established are also balanced to include all areas of my life: my relationships, physical being, and spiritual being. In the morning, before putting my feet on the floor, I review my vision and have a picture slideshow of everything in my vision of what I want. I immediately follow that with everything that I am thankful for. That balance that I create before allowing myself to get out of bed is the foundation for my day. Exercise for the wellness of both my body and mind ensures that I am in sync with the natural flow of life.

A healthy, active lifestyle is very important to me because it brings a healthy balance to my body. But through a very intense and long recovery from my shoulder surgery, for some time physical therapy and home exercises were the only forms of fitness that I was able to include in my fitness regime—that, and walking my dog. I was very happy when I was able to finally transition to the regular fitness modes that I enjoy. While I finally developed the endurance to get out hiking with Colby, getting back to the level of fitness I enjoyed previous to my shoulder injury took some time. I was overjoyed when my body started to heal enough to resume an exercise that I have enjoyed for more than fifteen years: Pilates! Pilates brings an inner balance that integrates tranquility to my body, mind, and spirit and combines meditation and strengthening of my body concurrently. I focus on my thoughts being positive as the gentle movements bring strength and conditioning to my body and make me stronger as a complete unit. I feel that balance when I step onto my reformer (the Pilates workout machine). I initially got into Pilates for core strengthening, which is great for my back. But I have gotten so much more out of this form of exercise. Pilates is now an experience for me, not a workout. It is the foundation that makes all of my parts harmonious.

The unity of balance within my body, mind, and spirit that Pilates gifts me, together with the balance of my life that this journey has brought, has me now in a place of complete harmony.

CONCLUSION

AFTER GOING THROUGH MY JOURNEY of self-realization and personal growth, I am more confident. I feel the confidence that I had when I went back to school more than ten years ago. I have finally stepped into the person that I was meant to be. I stand tall and bright. While I do not care to "stand out in a crowd," I feel like I ignited a light inside of me that comes out. That light is shining through me in my confidence. Before this time, I never thought to dream big. But with my growth and advancement, I have the confidence not only to set my goals high, but to know that I will achieve them. My confidence is exhibited to the world through my positive, confident, happy, and content energy. That is the way I prefer to stand out.

In my thoughts and feelings, I am unlimited. This period of time has allowed me to release and detach myself permanently from those thoughts and feelings that were bringing me down and holding me back and has brought me to a brand new pedestal on which I now stand. I feel unlimited in every way, from the amount of money I can earn, to what I can be, to what I can achieve. My goals and my aspirations are big, as they should be!

This huge change in my life came about thanks to my layoff and the time it gave me to navigate my way to a new existence. Permission to trust, acceptance of my situation, gratitude for what I had, meditation, making time for fun, following nudges from the universe, releasing limitations, concentrating on growth and advancement, finding my passions and purpose, defining my destiny, creating goals, setting intentions, making positive affirmations, and creating balance were stops along my way that culminated in my reach to the top of the mountain. I hope that what I have learned on this journey will help others on their own journeys.

ACKNOWLEDGEMENTS

Writing about my brother Frankie in this book made me remember and appreciate how big and full he lived in his sixteen years of life. He lived his life with a passion for everything he did and accomplished so much in such a short period of time. Frankie, your adventurous zest for life, positive outlook toward everything you did, and always reaching for the stars inspires me to live by your example. You are so missed but your memory lives on in me and those who loved you.

To my daughter, you are beautiful and strong and an inspiration for me to live with confidence to chase my dreams. I am so happy over the last year that we strengthened our bond and reconnected as a family. I love you more than you could ever know and I look forward to more fun adventures together.

To my beta readers, my daughter, Erica, and friends Lisa, Laura, Ann, Darlyne, and Toni, thank you for taking the time and making the effort to read my manuscript drafts and giving me your comments and feedback. Your input was invaluable to me. Thank you for cheering me on during the process.

To my editor, Skye Loyd, When I first found your website, I knew you were the right editor to help me bring my manuscript to life in a book. Thank you for guiding a new writer through your edits, direction, gentle nudges, and advice. As well, I am grateful for you recommending my designer. I appreciate all that you did for my manuscript.

To my book designer, Alan Barnett, thank you for guiding a new writer through the design and self-publishing process. Before I even committed, you had a vision for my manuscript. I am grateful for your patience in selecting a cover design. You made the process of all parts of the design easy for me to understand. Thank you for making the cover and inside of my book to be so much more than I ever imagined. I appreciate all of your efforts.

Thank you to the writings of Rhonda Byrne which inspired me to see the value in the practice of gratitude. Gratitude began this journey and continues to be one of the cornerstones of my life.

To the rest of my family and friends, thank you for being an incredible support system. Your unconditional love and kindness means the world to me.

There is so much good in my life, but the best parts of my life are the people and a very special canine in it. I am thankful for each of you.

Made in the USA
Middletown, DE
18 July 2021